W9-DCW-369

SCHOLASTIC ★ EXPLAINS™

READING HOMEWORK

SCHOLASTIC REFERENCE

Produced by Kirchoff/Wohlberg, Inc.
Editorial Director, Mary Jane Martin

CREDITS

Design and Electronic Production: Kirchoff/Wohlberg, Inc.

Illustration: Jared Lee, 6, 14, 15; Liz Callen, 10, 26, 27; Diane Paterson, 10, 33; Andy San Diego, 11; Don Madden, 11, 14, 58; Gail Piazza, 11, 35; Arvis Stewart, 12, 13; Betsy Day, 22; Eileen Hine, 46, 47; Michael Grejniec, 48, 49; John Wallner, 56, 57; Rosekrans Hoffman, 60; Gloria Elliot, 61; Andrea Wallace, 62, Tom Leonard, 25, 30, 41, 47.

Photo Acknowledgments: Page 3, PhotoDisc; Page 4, F. Stuart Westmorland/Photo Researchers; Page 5, Tim Davis/Photo Researchers; Page 6, Tony Freeman/PhotoEdit; Page 7, Ted Horowitz/The Stock Market; Page 8, Ted Horowitz/The Stock Market; Page 16, David Fleetham/FPG International; Page 17, Kevin Fall; Page 18, Kim Golding/ Tony Stone Images; Page 19, Garry Gray/The Image Bank; Page 20, The Kobal Collection; Page 21 (TOP), NASA; Page 21 (BOTTOM), Michelle Burgess/The Stock Market; Page 22 (BOTTOM RIGHT), From *The Magic School Bus Inside The Human Body* by Joanna Cole, illustrated by Bruce Degen. Illustrations copyright © 1989 by Bruce Degen. Reprinted by permission of Scholastic Inc. *The Magic School Bus* is a registered trademark of Scholastic Inc.; Page 23 (TOP), Text copyright 1935 by Laura Ingalls Wilder, copyright © renewed 1963 by Roger L. Macbride. Used by permission of HarperCollins Publishers. Please note: *Little House ®* is a Registered Trademark of HarperCollins Publishers, Inc.; Page 23 (MIDDLE), Reprinted with the permission of Simon & Schuster Books for Young Readers, an imprint of Simon & Schuster Children's Publishing Division from *Henry and Mudge and the Careful Cousin* by Cynthia Rylant, pictures by Suçie Stevenson. Jacket illustration copyright © 1994 Suçie Stevenson; Page 23 (BOTTOM), copyright © 1966 by Donald J. Sobol. Cover art copyright © 1994 by Eric Velasquez. Reprinted with the permission of Lodestar Books, a division of E.P. Dutton, a division of Penguin Books USA; Page 24 (BACK-GROUND), Library of Congress/ Corbis; Page 24 (TOP), Library of Congress; Page 24 (BOTTOM), UPI/Corbis-Bettmann; Page 25 (TOP), Guido Alberto Rossi/The Image Bank; Page 25 (BOTTOM), Ken Murray/ Daily News; Page 26, PhotoDisc; Page 28-29, From *Scholastic Children's Dictionary.* Copyright © 1996 by Scholastic, Inc.; Page 30 (BACKGROUND), NASA; Page 31 (TOP), Peter Beck/The Stock Market; Page 32, Wayne Newton/PhotoEdit; Page 34, Reprinted with the permission of Simon & Schuster Books for Young Readers, an imprint of Simon & Schuster Children's Publishing Division from *Night Songs* by Anne Miranda. Copyright © 1993 Anne Miranda; Page 36, Jeffrey Sylvester/FPG International; Page 37, Peter Beck/The Stock Market; Page 38-39, Reprinted with the permission of Simon & Schuster Books for Young Readers, an imprint of Simon & Schuster Children's Publishing Division from *Henry and Mudge and the Wild Wind* by Cynthia Rylant, pictures by Suçie Stevenson. Illustrations copyright © 1993 Suçie Stevenson; Page 40, Paul Barton/The Stock Market; Page 42 (BACKGROUND), California Institute of Technology; Page 42 (INSET), NASA; Page 43, Adapted from *A Book about Planets and Stars* by Betty Polisar Reigot. Copyright © 1988 by Betty Polisar Reigot. Reprinted by permission of Scholastic Inc.; Page 43 (LEFT), NASA; Page 43 (RIGHT), California Institute of Technology; Page 44, F. Stuart Westmorland/Photo Researchers; Page 45, Tim Davis/Photo Researchers; Page 50, Kevin Fall; Page 51, Kathy Bushue/Tony Stone Images; Page 52, Mindy E. Klarman/Photo Researchers; Page 53, Mindy E. Klarman/Photo Researchers; Page 54, W. Eastep/The Stock Market; Page 59, Copyright © 1994 Ladybird Books Ltd.; Page 61, Photos © John Lei; Page 62, From *Amelia Bedelia and the Baby.* Illustrations copyright © 1981 by Lynn Sweat. By permission of Greenwillow Books, a division of William Morrow and Company; Page 63, Bryan F. Peterson/The Stock Market.

Board of Advisors

Dale Beltzner
Liberty Bell Elementary School
Coopersburg, Pennsylvania

Beverly Wilson
John R. Good School
Irving, Texas

Linda Neth
Groveport Elementary School
Groveport, Ohio

Allan Yeager
Richard Crane Elementary School
Rohnert Park, California

No part of this publication may be reproduced in whole or in part, or stored in a retrieval system, or transmitted in any form or by any means, electronic, mechanical, photocopying, recording, or otherwise, without written permission of the publisher. For information regarding permissions, write to Permissions Department, Scholastic Inc., 555 Broadway, New York, NY 10012.

Library of Congress Cataloging-in-Publication Data

Scholastic explains reading homework: everything children (and parents) need to survive 2nd and 3rd grades.
p. cm. (Scholastic explains homework series.)

Summary: Discusses the ways books and different kinds of writing are organized and how to get the most out of reading for pleasure and for information.
ISBN 0-590-39755-9 (hardcover).   ISBN 0-590-39758-3 (pbk.)

1. Reading (Primary)—United States—Juvenile literature. 2. Homework—Juvenile literature.
[1. Books and reading.] I. Scholastic Inc. II. Title: Reading homework   III. Series
LB1525.S345 1998   372.41'2–dc21   97-41137   CIP   AC

Copyright © 1998 by Scholastic Inc.

All rights reserved. Published by Scholastic Inc.
SCHOLASTIC, SCHOLASTIC EXPLAINS, and associated logos are trademarks and/or registered trademarks of Scholastic Inc.
Printed in the U.S.A.   14
First Scholastic printing, August 1998
8 7 6 5   2 3 4 5 0/0

Table of  Contents

Here's How It Works 4

Here's How It Works

A Note to Parents

Your child is hard at work on reading homework. Everything seems fine. But then comes that moan of frustration. This kid needs help.

You may not have written about an author's purpose in a good many years, and you may never have used a graphic organizer. The homework instructions may be hard to understand, incompletely copied, or just plain missing. That's where this book comes in.

Begin by looking through the table of contents with your child to get an overview of the subjects that are included. Ask your child which topics seem familiar. Knowing what your child knows will help you to help your child with homework problems.

To find a particular topic, look at the index. You can look up the assignment subject using the word your child uses (*order*, for example) or the term you remember (*sequence*). Either way will lead you to the right pages. Then just work with your child, reading a definition, sharing examples, or following instructions as needed.

At right is a guide to two typical pages from *Scholastic Explains Reading Homework*, with the elements you will find throughout the book.

That's all there is to it. Happy homework!

basic definition in language used in the classroom

homework subject

expanded definition

What's the BIG Idea?

IDENTIFY MAIN IDEA AND DETAILS

The **main idea** is the most important idea of a paragraph. **Details** are sentences that tell about the main idea.

Sometimes the main idea is **stated** in a sentence at the beginning or the end of a paragraph.

DOLPHIN SOUNDS

Dolphins use sounds to talk with one another. They make whistles, squeaks, and clicks. Scientists study dolphin noises by listening to the patterns of their sounds. They have discovered that each dolphin has a sound of its own that other dolphins use to call it.

The main idea is stated in the first sentence.

Here's a **web** that shows the main idea and details.

Detail
Dolphins make whistles, clicks, and squeaks.

Main Idea
Dolphins use sounds to talk with one another.

Detail
Each dolphin has a sound of its own that other dolphins use to call it.

Detail
Scientists study dolphin noises.

44

sample paragraph

example

find topics in ABC order at the end of the book, on page 64

expanded definition

Index

Sometimes a paragraph is made up of details about the main idea, but the main idea is **unstated**. The reader needs to look at the detail sentences and figure out the main idea.

Dolphins can tell whether something is near or far away. They talk to other dolphins. They sense when there is danger.

The main idea is not stated.

Detail
They talk to other dolphins.

Main Idea
Dolphins know many things.

Detail
Dolphins can tell whether something is near or far away.

Detail
They sense when there is danger.

example

sample paragraph

EXTRA HELP

When you read, ask yourself these questions:
What are most of the sentences in the paragraph about?
Is there a sentence that tells the main idea?
Which sentences tell about the main idea?

NOTE
The **topic** of the two paragraphs on these pages is dolphins. Sometimes the topic is called the **subject**.

other vocabulary used by teachers

ideas to use to do an assignment

45

Inside and Out

PARTS OF A BOOK

Books have special parts that give you different kinds of information.

Before you even open a book, you can learn about it.

front cover

Best Jokes Ever

written by James Stuart
pictures by Mary Stone

author
title   illustrator

back cover

About the Book
You will laugh for hours when you read these hilarious jokes.

why you should read the book

There is more information on the **front pages**.

title page

Best Jokes Ever

written by
James Stuart

pictures by
Mary Stone

Reader's
Publishing Co.

author
title
illustrator
publisher's name

copyright page

Copyright © 1998

year published
author, illustrator, or publisher may hold the copyright

dedication

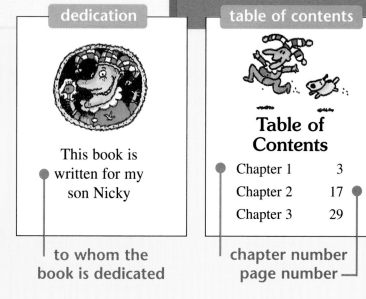

This book is written for my son Nicky

to whom the book is dedicated

table of contents

Table of Contents

Chapter 1   3
Chapter 2   17
Chapter 3   29

chapter number
page number

Special Sections

At the **back** of nonfiction books, you may find these special sections.

index page

Index

bats, 5

caps, 7, 9, 19

cards, 22

fields, 4, 10

home run, 15

players, 20–22

rules, 29–35

glossary page

Glossary

base: one of four corners on a baseball field diamond where the runners go in order to score

mitt: leather glove used for protection when playing baseball

An **index** is an alphabetical list that tells on which pages you can find a particular topic.

A **glossary** is an alphabetical list that gives the meanings of some words used in the book.

 NOTE

Some books have **book jackets**. On the front flap is a summary of the book. On the back flap is information about the author.

What Do You Want to Know? →	Where to Look
What is the title?	cover, title page
On which page does Chapter 3 begin?	table of contents
What is the meaning of *outfield*?	glossary
When was this book published?	copyright page
On which page will I find information about caps?	index

What's That Word?

LETTERS AND SOUNDS

When you read, you may come
to a word you don't recognize.

Billy read this:

You will see many **frogs** in a pond like this
one. You might also see a **salamander**
climbing up on the rocks to sit in the sun.

Billy thought this . . .

I don't know this word. I'll skip it. No,
I can figure it out. It begins like *salad*–**sal**.
Next I see *a*. I know *a* sometimes spells the
sound **uh**. Next I see *man* and I know it says
man. The word ends like *spider*–**dur**. Let's see:
sal-uh-man-dur. *Salamander*! I know that word.
A salamander looks like a lizard.

If you come to a word
you don't know, try this:

- Look at the letters.
- Sound out the word.

  Think about the sounds
  the consonant letters
  usually stand for in a
  word you know.

  Try short sounds for the
  vowels you see.

  Try long sounds for the
  vowels you see.

  Try the sound *uh* for the
  vowels you see.

- Then say the word in
  the sentence to see if it
  makes sense.

Letters to Look Out For

Some words may surprise you.
Here are some spellings to look out for.

ph spells /**f**/

phone
photo
graph
nephew

gh may spell /**f**/, too

tough
rough
enough
laugh

k is silent when it comes before the letter **n**

knew
know
knob
knee

g is silent when it comes before the letter **n**

gnu
gnarl
gnash
gnat

ti sometimes spells /**sh**/

motion
direction
action
vacation

b is sometimes silent after the letter **m**

numb
climb
thumb
plumber

w is silent when it comes before the letter **r**

write
wrong
wrap
wrestle

Vowel Sounds

Here are the vowel sounds and their spellings.

/a/   mad, pat
/ah/   father
/air/   fair, care
/ar/   dark
/ay/   pay, claim
      (a-*consonant*-e) made, nape
/aw/   raw, caught
/e/   met, men
/ee/   beet
/i/   bit, accident
/ihr/   fear, here
/eye/   iron, rabbi, lie, my
      (i-*consonant*-e) file, ripe
      (*consonant*-ye) rye, dye
/o/   cot, dot
/oh/   foe, dough
      (o-*consonant*-e) alone, stone
/oo/   pool, rude
/or/   corn, more
/oi/   boil, toy
/ou/   how, ouch
/u/   put, book
/uh/   bun, comma
/ur/   burn, worker
/yoo/   music, pure

NOTE

An unaccented short **u** sound is called a **schwa** (ə). The last syllable in *lemon* and the first syllable in *ago* have a schwa sound.

Picture This!

READING PICTURE CLUES

In many books, **pictures** help to tell the story, so it's important to pay attention to them.

A picture can show you how a character feels.

"It's snail soup. Isn't it just the best thing you've ever eaten?"

"Oh, no!" said Mom. "Here comes Mary with her didgeridoo."

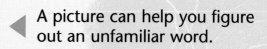
A picture can help you figure out an unfamiliar word.

Every summer, our family used to go to the seashore. For two weeks, we would live in a grand hotel.

There's More to the Story.

A picture can tell you the **setting**, where and when a story takes place.

"This is great!" thought Bunny. "I've never skated so fast before. Nothing can stop me now!"

"I'd like a pair of flippers, size extra large, please."

A picture can help you predict what is going to happen in the **plot**, the main story in the book.

A picture can let the reader in on a joke.

NOTE

For more about **setting** and **plot**, *see pp. 54–55 and pp. 38–39.*

What Makes Sense?

CONTEXT CLUES

The **context** of a word is the other words around it. The context can help you figure out what a word means.

Suppose you didn't know what the word *visible* meant in the story below. Here's how the context could help you.

The Emperor's New Clothes

The Emperor greeted the weaver at the palace.

"Soon the cloth for your suit will be ready," said the weaver. "It is the most beautiful cloth in the world."

The Emperor couldn't wait to see it.

"But remember," said the weaver, "this cloth is only *visible* to those who are smart. Only the smart people of your kingdom will be able to see the cloth, but those who are not smart won't be able to see it."

Look at the word *visible* and then at the next sentence. It says that only smart people will be able to see the cloth. The word *visible* probably means "something that can be seen." It makes sense in the sentence. The cloth can only be seen by those who are smart.

Here's how the context can help you to figure out the meaning of the word *exquisite*.

At last, the suit was ready.

"Here is your suit," said the weaver. He lifted his arms toward the Emperor.

But to the Emperor's surprise, he saw nothing! Of course, he did not want anyone to think that he was not smart, so the Emperor pretended he could see the new suit.

"How *exquisite*!" he shouted. "It is truly beautiful!"

Read the word *exquisite* and the sentence that follows it. It says that the Emperor said that the cloth was truly beautiful. The word *exquisite* probably means "truly beautiful." That makes sense.

EXTRA HELP

When you come to a word or phrase you don't know, do this:

- Read the words near the word you don't know. You might find the same idea written another way.
- Look at the picture for a clue.
- If you're still unsure, look up the word in a dictionary.
  (See pp. 28–29.)

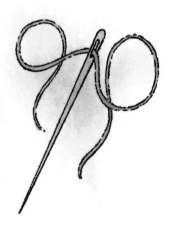

Did You Really Mean That?

MULTIPLE-MEANING WORDS

Some words look exactly the same, but they have different meanings. They are called multiple-meaning words.

Often jokes are written with words that have multiple meanings. Here's a joke that is funny because there are two meanings for the word *dressing*.

What did the mayonnaise say to the refrigerator?

"Close the door, I'm dressing!"

If you think that the word *dressing* means "putting on clothes," instead of "a sauce to put on salad," this becomes very funny to think about and picture in your mind.

Read this joke and think about the two meanings for the word *bark*.

What is the noisiest part of a tree? The bark.

Now read this one and think about two meanings for *stories*.

Why is a tall building like a book of fairy tales?

It has lots of stories.

NOTE

Words that are spelled the same but have different meanings are also called **homographs**.

DON'T BE CONFUSED!

When you read, make sure to think about what you are reading so that you understand which meaning of the word the author is using.

band — The *band* played a march.
Put a rubber *band* around the pencils.

ring — I have a new *ring*.
The phone began to *ring*.

count — The *count* wore purple.
I can *count* to 60.

mean — The dog did not look *mean*.
What does this sign *mean*?

seal — The envelope has a *seal*.
That *seal* clapped its flippers.

pitcher — The *pitcher* threw the ball.
The milk is in a *pitcher*.

bow — Her *bow* was red and white.
The arrow is for the *bow*.

EXTRA HELP

If a word doesn't seem to make sense the way it is used in the sentence, look it up. The word may have more than one meaning.

Beginnings and Endings

PREFIXES AND SUFFIXES

A prefix or a suffix is a word part that changes the meaning of a base word.

> A **prefix** is added to the beginning of a word. When you read, notice how the meaning of the word changes when a prefix is added.

PREFIXES

un means not
uncovered	not covered
unhappy	not happy
unkind	not kind

Marine Animals

If you were to go on a **marine** trip, you might go in a **submarine**. You might see **usual** and **unusual** animals. There are many fish that are **like** each other, but with its eight arms, an octopus is **unlike** any other sea creature.

submarine = goes under the sea
unusual = not usual
unlike = not like

re means again
rebuild	build again
rethink	think again
redo	do again

dis means not, lack of, or take away
disagree	not agree
disrespect	lack of respect
disconnect	to take away the connection

tri means three
triangle	shape with three angles
tricycle	cycle with three wheels

pre means before
prepay	pay ahead of time
preschool	before grade school
preview	before viewing

sub means under
subway	underground train
submerge	to place under water
subfreezing	under the freezing point

A **suffix** is added to the end of a word. When you read, notice how the meaning of the word changes when a suffix is added.

Taking Care of Shells

Many people **collect** shells. Shell **collectors** like to show off their shells. Shells have to be handled with **care**. If someone is **careless**, a shell can break. It is good to **separate** shells and display them **separately**, so that they don't hit one another and break.

collect**or** = one who collects

care**less** = without care

separate**ly** = in a separate way

SUFFIXES

less means *without*

helpless	without help
homeless	without a home
thoughtless	without thought

ful means *full of, with*

careful	with care
thankful	full of thanks
thoughtful	with thought

ist means *one who makes or plays*

artist	one who makes art
pianist	one who plays piano
violinist	one who plays violin

or (er) means *one who does*

actor	one who acts
editor	one who edits
singer	one who sings

ly means *in a certain way*

kindly	in a kind way
happily	in a happy way
sadly	in a sad way

ward means *toward*

eastward	toward the east
westward	toward the west
backward	toward the back

NOTE

A **base** word is sometimes called a **root** word.

Sound Surprises

RHYMING WORDS

Words that have the same ending sounds are rhyming words.

When the endings of **rhyming words** are spelled the same, it is easy to read them.

cat   sat   hat   mat

track

sack

Jack

ox

box

fox

Rhyme Time

Sometimes words that rhyme have spellings that may surprise you.

noodle
strudel

came
aim

daughter
water

my
tie
high
rye

head
fed
said

of
love

NOTE

The words *a* and *the* often rhyme with each other.

nut
what

after
laughter

late
eight

doze
pose

your
you're
sure

to
gnu
few
too
true
two

they
may

quite
sight

are
car

were
stir
fur

all
crawl
haul

put
foot

weak
seek

row
toe
dough

bought
caught

heard
bird
word
purred
curd

leaf
brief

for
pour
more

19

Did It Really Happen?

FICTION AND NONFICTION

When you read, the writing may be **fiction** or **nonfiction**.

Fiction is writing that tells about things that did not really happen. Fiction is made up by the author.

There are many kinds of fiction.

Mystery Stories

Science Fiction

Humorous Fiction

Tall Tales

Fantasy

Fiction

Realistic Fiction

Historical Fiction

Folktales

Fables

Nonfiction is about people, places, and things that are real. Nonfiction tells about something that is true.

There are many kinds of nonfiction.

How-to Books

Newspaper Articles

Informational Books

Nonfiction

Autobiographies

Biographies

Magazine Articles

Moonwalk, *Apollo 17*

Serengeti National Park, Tanzania

EXTRA HELP

Don't be fooled! Sometimes fiction can seem very real. When you read, ask yourself: Did this happen or did the author make it up?

Let's Pretend

A WORLD OF FICTION

You probably read lots of **fiction**. Writers of fiction tell stories about things that did not really happen.

Fantasy

Fiction that seems unbelievable is called **fantasy**.

In fantasy, things happen that couldn't possibly happen in the real world.

- Fantasy characters are unlike real people and animals. You might meet a giant or a talking fish.

- A fantasy setting may be very different from the real world. You might find yourself in a kingdom under the sea or on a cloud in the sky.

There are different kinds of fantasy stories.

In a **fable**, the characters learn an important lesson. Often the characters are animals that act like people. "The Lion and the Mouse" is an example of a fable.

In a **folktale**, the good characters usually win. Sometimes a folktale reflects a certain country or culture. "Three Little Pigs" and "The Goose That Laid the Golden Egg" are folktales.

In a **tall tale**, the characters are exaggerated, larger than life. The setting is the past or the future. "Paul Bunyan" is a tall tale.

In **science fiction**, the ideas are based on real or imagined information from the field of science or technology. The setting can be the past, present or future. *The Magic School Bus* books are science fiction.

Realistic Fiction

Fiction that seems real is called realistic fiction.

In realistic fiction things happen as they might in real life.

- The characters act as they might in real life.
- The setting seems real.
- The action takes place in the present or past.

There are different kinds of realistic fiction.

In **historical fiction**, the setting is always a past time. Characters act like they might have in that time and place, and things happen as they might have then. Sometimes the characters are based on real people and events. The *Little House* books are examples of historical fiction.

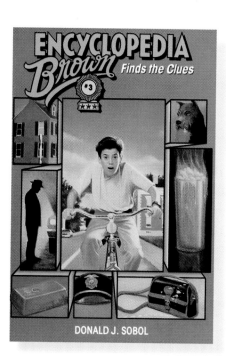

In a **mystery story**, a series of clues is given to help the characters, and the reader, solve a problem. For example, the *Encyclopedia Brown* books are mystery stories.

In **humorous fiction**, the characters do funny things that may surprise you. Sometimes what happens is exaggerated to make it seem funnier. The books about *Henry and Mudge* are examples of humorous fiction.

NOTE

A story can be more than one kind of fiction.

Let's Be Real!

A WORLD OF NONFICTION

You have probably read many kinds of nonfiction. **Nonfiction** is filled with information about people, places and things that are real.

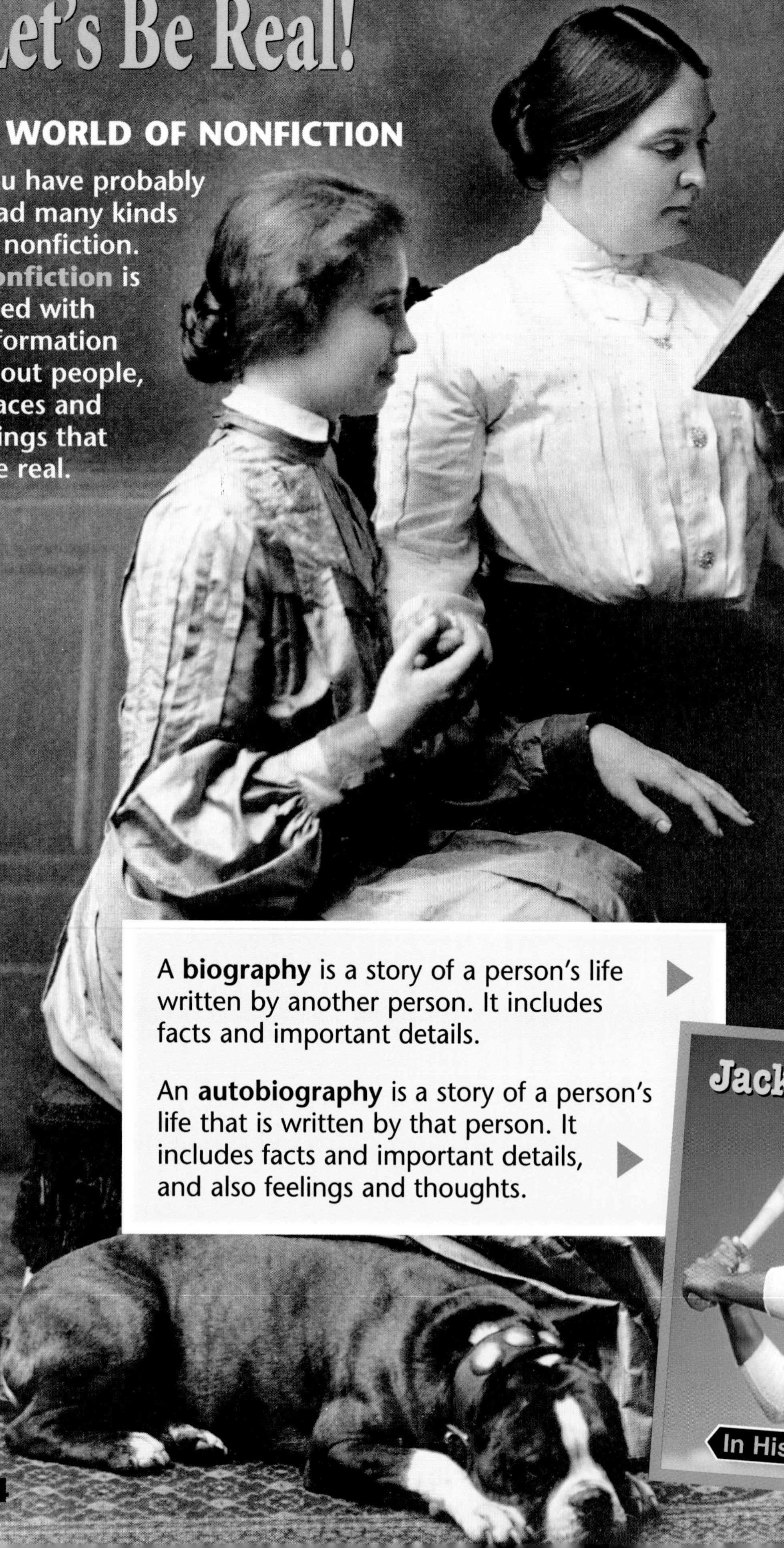

Helen Keller and Annie Sullivan

A **biography** is a story of a person's life written by another person. It includes facts and important details. ▶

An **autobiography** is a story of a person's life that is written by that person. It includes facts and important details, and also feelings and thoughts. ▶

George Washington

written by M. J. Evans

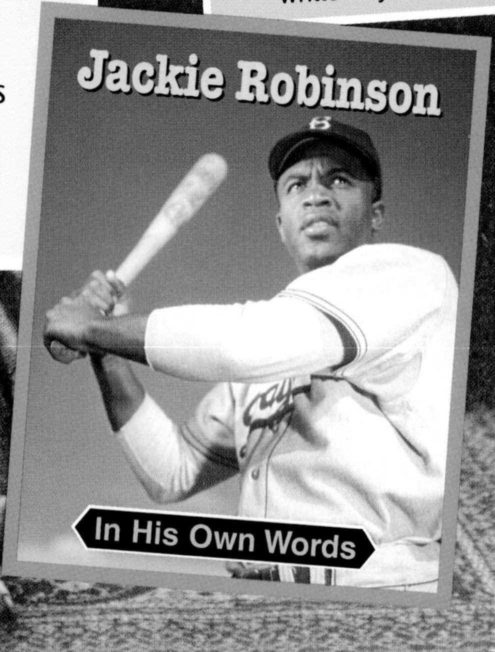

Jackie Robinson

In His Own Words

24

Reading Nonfiction

Look through the table of contents to see how the book is organized. Use the index at the back of the book to locate information you want. Also, glossary pages give definitions of special words.

An **informational book** contains facts and information about one particular topic. Sometimes the information is told as a story. The chapter titles and headings help the reader find information.

A **how-to book** gives the reader information on how to do or make something. The steps are given in order and may be numbered. Sometimes diagrams are included.

A **newspaper article** or a **magazine article** has a headline that tells what the article is about. The body of the article includes details, facts, and information.

The Five W's

A good newspaper story answers five **w** questions:

Who is the story about?

What happened?

When did it happen?

Where did it happen?

Why did it happen?

Where to Find It

REFERENCE SOURCES

There is so much information in the world that nobody can possibly know it all. It is important to know where to look for the information you want or need to know.

A Dictionary

A dictionary shows how a word is spelled, how it is pronounced, and what it means.

An Encyclopedia

An encyclopedia has information about all kinds of topics. There is a brief article about each one. Most encyclopedias are sets of books. Some are on **CD-ROM**, so you can use them on the computer.

NOTE

Atlases and dictionaries are on CD-ROM, too.

I wanted to know what talon means, so I looked it up in a dictionary. I found out that it is the sharp claw of a bird of prey.

I wanted to know if bears are vegetarians, so I looked up bears in an encyclopedia.

I used the encyclopedia on my computer.

Read All About It

My best friend is moving to Albuquerque, New Mexico. I wanted to know where that is, so I looked in an atlas.

An Atlas

An atlas has maps and mileage charts. It shows where oceans, countries, states, cities, rivers, and mountains are located.

I wanted to find another word for smart, so I looked it up in a thesaurus.

A Thesaurus

Look in a thesaurus to find *synonyms*. Synonyms are words that have similar meanings, such as *happy* and *delighted*. A thesaurus also has *antonyms*. Antonyms are words that have opposite meanings, such as *happy* and *miserable*.

I wanted to know about sled dogs. I found this book about all kinds of dogs.

Nonfiction Books

A nonfiction book contains information about a topic.

We wanted to make a birdhouse, so we found a video to show us how to do it.

Videos

Videos can be very helpful if you want to learn how to do something because they can tell you how *and* show you how.

NOTE

Most reference books are in ABC order.

27

Words and More Words

USING A DICTIONARY

When you read, you may come to a word you don't know. You can use a **dictionary** to find out the meaning of a word and how to say it. Here are some hints to help you read the dictionary.

Pronunciations, given in parentheses, follow most entry words.

Guide Words tell you the first and last entry words on the page. **Spectacles** is the first word, and **sphinx** is the last word on this page.

Entry Words are in dark type and are in alphabetical order. The order helps you find a word. Some words have more than one meaning. Each meaning is next to a number under the entry. Some entries have illustrations.

Syllable Breaks are shown by small dots. In many dictionaries, entries made up of two separate words, or two words with a hyphen, are not broken into syllables.

---

spectacles ▶ sphinx

spec·ta·cles (spek-tuh-kuhlz) *noun, plural*
Eyeglasses.

spec·tac·u·lar (spek-tak-yuh-lur) *adjective*
Remarkable or dramatic, as in *a spectacular sunset.* ▷ *adverb* **spectacularly**

spec·ta·tor (spek-tay-tur) *noun* Someone who watches an event and does not participate in it.
▷ *adjective* **spectator**

spec·ter (spek-tur) *noun* A ghost. ▷ *adjective* **spectral**

spec·trum (spek-truhm) *noun*
1. The range of colors that is revealed when light shines through a prism or through drops of water, as in a rainbow. *When white light travels through a prism, it is refracted, or bent. Since each of the colors in light travels at a slightly different speed, each bends at a different angle and the range of colors spreads out in a spectrum.*
2. A wide range of things or ideas.
▷ *noun, plural* **spectrums** or **spectra** (spek-truh)

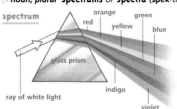

spectrum — ray of white light — glass prism — red, orange, yellow, green, blue, indigo, violet

spec·u·late (spek-yuh-late) *verb*
1. To wonder or guess about something without knowing all the facts.
2. To invest in something that is risky, such as a business or a stock.
▷ *verb* **speculating, speculated** ▷ *noun* **speculation, ** *noun* **speculator**

speech (speech) *noun*
1. The ability to speak.
2. A talk given to a group of people. ▷ *noun, plural* **speeches**
3. The way in which someone speaks. *I can tell by your speech that you're from the South.*

speech·less (speech-liss) *adjective* Unable to speak. *He was speechless with rage.*

speed (speed)
1. *noun* The rate at which something moves.
2. *noun* The rate of any action. *I'm taking a class to improve my reading speed.*
3. *verb* To travel very fast or faster than is allowed. ▷ **speeding, sped** (sped) or **speeded**
4. *noun* Quickness of movement.

speed bump *noun* A ridge of asphalt or hard rubber that has been laid across a road or parking lot to make drivers slow down.

speed·om·e·ter (spi-dom-uh-tur) *noun* An instrument in a vehicle that shows how fast you are traveling. *See* **motorcycle.**

spell (spel)
1. *verb* To write or say the letters of a word in their correct order.
2. *verb* To mean. *The captain's injury spelled trouble for the team.*
3. *verb* To take someone's place for a time. *During our cross-country car trip, my parents spelled each other at the wheel.*
4. *noun* A period of time, usually a short one, as in *a spell of rainy weather.*
5. *noun* A word or words supposed to have magical powers.
6. *verb* If you **spell out** an idea or a plan, you explain it clearly and in detail.
▷ *verb* **spelling, spelled**

spell checker *noun* A computer program that searches for misspelled words by comparing each word in a document to correctly spelled words.

spe·lunk·ing (spi-luhng-king) *noun* If you go **spelunking,** you explore caves. ▷ *noun* **spelunker**

spend (spend) *verb*
1. To use money to buy things.
2. To pass time. *We will spend our vacation at the beach.*
3. If you **spend** time or energy, you use it.
▷ *verb* **spending, spent** (spent)

sperm (spurm) *noun* One of the reproductive cells from a male that is capable of fertilizing eggs in a female.

sphere (sfihr) *noun*
1. A solid shape like a basketball or globe, with all points of the shape the same distance from the center of the shape. ▷ *adjective* **spherical** (sfihr-uh-kuhl or sfer-uh-kuhl)
2. An area of activity, interest, or knowledge. *Poetry is in my sphere of interest.*

sphinx (sfingks) *noun*
1. In Egyptian mythology, a creature with the body of a lion and the head of a man, ram, or hawk.
2. **the Sphinx** A large statue of this creature in Giza, Egypt.
▷ *noun, plural* **sphinxes**

the Sphinx

512

28

Part of Speech labels tell that a word is a noun, a verb, an adjective, an adverb, or another part of speech.

Labeled Illustrations show you additional information about entry words.

Definitions tell the meanings of entry words.

Related Words and Word Forms are at the end of an entry or at the end of a meaning.

Sample Sentences follow some of the meanings. These sentences show how the word is used.

Cross References tell you where in the dictionary to find more information about the entry word.

spice ▶ spinal cord

spice (spisse) *noun*
1. A substance with a distinctive smell or taste used to flavor foods. *The picture shows a range of spices.*
2. Anything that adds excitement or interest. *Variety is the spice of life.* ▷ *verb* **spice**

spices

cloves

powdered turmeric

paprika

caraway seeds

nutmeg

cinnamon sticks

allspice

cumin seeds

spi·cy (spye-see) *adjective* Containing lots of spices; having a pungent taste. *My father makes very spicy chili.* ▷ **spicier, spiciest**

spi·der (spye-dur) *noun* A small animal with eight legs, a body divided into two parts, and no wings. Spiders spin webs to trap insects for food. *The picture shows a selection of spiders from around the world.*

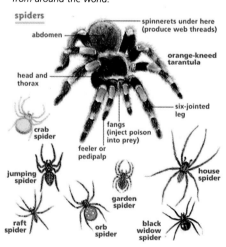

spiders

abdomen

spinnerets under here (produce web threads)

orange-kneed tarantula

head and thorax

six-jointed leg

crab spider

fangs (inject poison into prey)

feeler or pedipalp

jumping spider

garden spider

house spider

raft spider

orb spider

black widow spider

spike (spike)
1. *noun* A large, heavy nail often used to fasten rails to railroad ties. ▷ *verb* **spike**
2. *noun* A pointed piece of metal attached to the sole of a shoe to help athletes get and keep firm footing.
3. *noun* An ear of wheat or grain, such as corn.
4. *noun* A long cluster of flowers on one stem.
5. *verb* To hit a volleyball down and over the net with force so that it is difficult to return.
▷ **spiking, spiked**
▷ *noun* **spike** ▷ *adjective* **spiked**

spill (spil)
1. *verb* If you **spill** something, you let the contents of a container fall out, often accidentally.
2. *verb* To run out or flow over. *Tears spilled from her eyes.*
3. *noun* A serious fall. *Mike took a bad spill off his motorcycle.*
▷ *verb* **spilling, spilled** *or* **spilt** (spilt)

spin (spin)
1. *verb* To make thread by twisting fine fibers together. *The picture shows a spinning jenny, a machine invented in the 18th century that could spin up to eight threads at once.*

spinning jenny

2. *verb* To make a web or cocoon by giving off a liquid that hardens into thread. *Spiders spin webs.*
3. *verb* To rotate or to whirl around. *The earth spins.*
4. *verb* To tell or to relate. *The old sea captain spins a good tale.*
5. *verb* To feel dizzy, or as if your head is whirling around. *The roller coaster made my head spin.*
6. *noun* A short ride. *We took the new car out for a spin around the block.*
7. *noun* A special interpretation or point of view. *The senator put a positive spin on the poll results.*
▷ *verb* **spinning, spun** (spuhn)

spin·ach (spin-ich) *noun* A dark green, leafy vegetable. *See* **vegetable.**

spinal column *noun* A series of connected bones in your back that support and protect the spinal cord. Spinal column is another term for **backbone.**

spinal cord *noun* A thick cord of nerve tissue that starts at the brain and runs through the center of the spinal column. The spinal cord carries impulses to and from the brain and links the brain to the rest of the nerves in the body.

S

Where in the World?

READING A MAP

Maps are pictures. Most maps are pictures of part of the earth's surface.

The artist who plans a map is called a **cartographer**. The cartographer's job is to use symbols on the map that will tell you what that part of the earth's surface is like.

One map cannot tell you everything about a place. Different kinds of maps tell different information.

This **relief map** shows a lot about Colorado's surface.

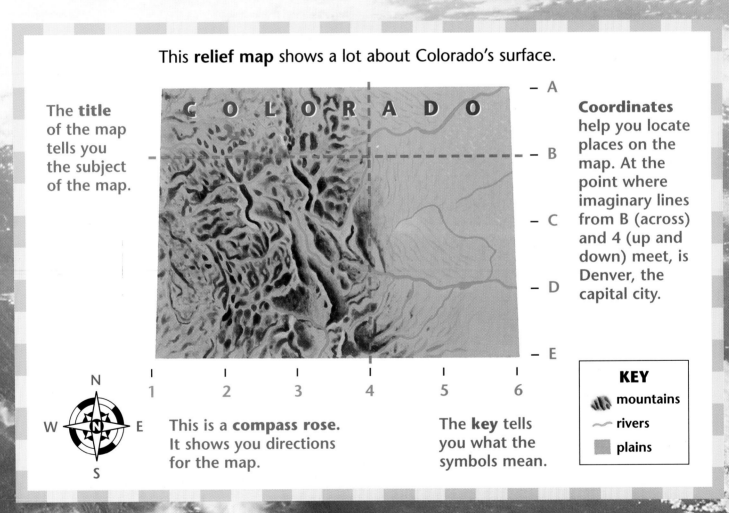

The **title** of the map tells you the subject of the map.

COLORADO

— A

— B

— C

— D

— E

1   2   3   4   5   6

Coordinates help you locate places on the map. At the point where imaginary lines from B (across) and 4 (up and down) meet, is Denver, the capital city.

N
W — E
S

This is a **compass rose**. It shows you directions for the map.

The **key** tells you what the symbols mean.

KEY

🐝 mountains

〜 rivers

▬ plains

Highways and Byways

The map on this page is a kind of **road map**. It shows you the main roads around Denver, Colorado. It also shows you Colorado cities and towns that are connected by these roads. Notice that this map does not show the whole state.

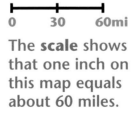

The **scale** shows that one inch on this map equals about 60 miles.

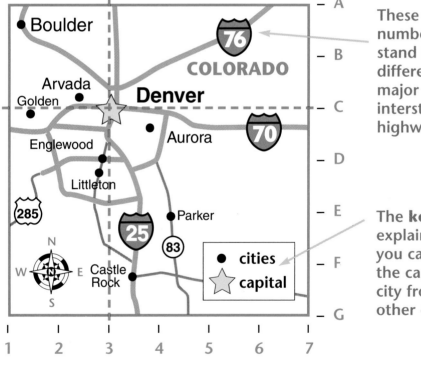

These numbers stand for different major interstate highways.

The **key** explains how you can tell the capital city from the other cities.

The numbers and the letters (coordinates) help you find places. Find Denver on this map. Then look at the relief map on p. 30. What might you see on a car trip that started in Denver and went west?

Here's How to Do It

READ AND FOLLOW DIRECTIONS

You **read directions** when you want to find out how to do or make something. You want to do it right, so reading the directions is important.

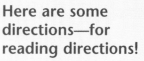

Here are some directions—for reading directions!

1. Read all the directions through first, before you start to follow them.

2. Be sure you have the materials and tools you need.

3. Think about what you will do at each step to make sure you understand what you have read.

4. Decide if you need help from a friend or an adult.

5. Keep directions close by so you can look at them as you go along. If they are long, use a sticky note to mark your place.

Make a Siphon

This shows what you might think as you follow directions.

1. Fill one bottle three-quarters full of water. Place both bottles on a flat surface. The filled bottle should be on a higher surface than the empty one.

2. Place one end of the tube in the bottle that has the water in it. Put the other end in your mouth and suck up the water until the tube is full.

3. Lift the bottle with the water in it and hold it just above your eye level. Stop sucking and quickly put your thumb over the end of the tube to keep the water from coming out.

4. Place the end of the tube you are holding in the empty bottle and take your thumb away.

5. Watch the water flow through the tube, from the upper bottle to the lower bottle. Water pressure drives it down the tube.

OK. I'VE GOT THIS STUFF.

WATER? I'LL NEED TO DO THIS IN THE KITCHEN SINK.

I'LL HAVE TO BE CAREFUL NOT TO SWALLOW IT. OH! IT'S JUST WATER.

I'LL MEMORIZE THIS. I CAN'T DO THIS AND READ AT THE SAME TIME.

I'LL HAVE TO TAKE MY THUMB AWAY FIRST.

HEY! IT WORKS!

Listen!

In a **poem**, words are chosen for their sounds as well as for their meanings.

Some poems do not rhyme. They are called **free verse**. Listen for the sounds in this poem about cows.

Cows

Cows huddle closely
in the grassy blackness
and low
as the crickets chirp
their scratchy meadow melody.
— *Anne Miranda*

Listen to the sounds of poetry. Some poems **rhyme**. Listen for rhyming words at the end of lines 2 and 4. Then read the poem again and clap the beat. The beat, or **rhythm**, can be regular as it is in **I'm Glad**. The rhythm can be irregular as it is in **Cows**.

Some poems have **alliteration**. Alliteration is the repetition of beginning sounds. Listen for the sounds that are alike.

I'm Glad

I'm glad the sky is painted blue,
   And the earth is painted green,
With such a lot of nice fresh air
   All sandwiched in between.
                              —*Anonymous*

Peter Piper

Peter Piper picked a peck of pickled peppers.
A peck of pickled peppers Peter Piper picked.
If Peter Piper picked a peck of pickled peppers,
How many pickled peppers did Peter Piper pick?
                              —*Anonymous*

Painting Pictures with Words

A poet uses words to help you form a picture in your mind.

Suppose a poet wanted you to know how quiet Jane was. The poet might compare Jane to a quiet mouse.

A **simile** compares two things using the words *as* or *like*.
As quiet as a mouse is a simile.

> Jane slipped slowly from her room,
> *As quiet as a mouse*.
> She went to find her teddy
> While everyone slept in the house.

A **metaphor** compares two things without using the words *as* or *like*.
Jane the mouse is a metaphor.

> *Jane the mouse* crept back to bed;
> She didn't make a sound.
> All tucked in warm, she fell asleep.
> Her teddy she had found.

EXTRA HELP

Now picture these!

Similes	Metaphors
as soft as a pillow	she is a treasure
sweet as candy	a sea of books
roaring like a lion	a world of toys

NOTE

Metaphors and similes are **figurative language.** Figurative language helps the reader see something in a new way.

So Much to Remember!

USE GRAPHIC ORGANIZERS

Here are some ways to help you remember what you read.

If you were reading about *Tyrannosaurus rex* and wanted to remember all about it, you might make a **list** of things you want to remember.

Tyrannosaurus rex

1. Tyrannosaurus was about 18 feet high.
2. It had huge jaws and sharp teeth.
3. Tyrannosaurus was a meat-eater.
4. Tyrannosaurus was the most ferocious dinosaur.
5. It weighed between 6 and 7 tons.
6. It was more than 40 feet long.
7. Tyrannosaurus had thick, muscled legs and clawed feet.

Or, you could make a **word web** about *T. rex*, like the one on the right.

thickly muscled legs and clawed feet

18 feet high

most ferocious

TYRANNOSAURUS

40 feet long

meat-eater

huge jaws and sharp teeth

weighed 6-7 tons

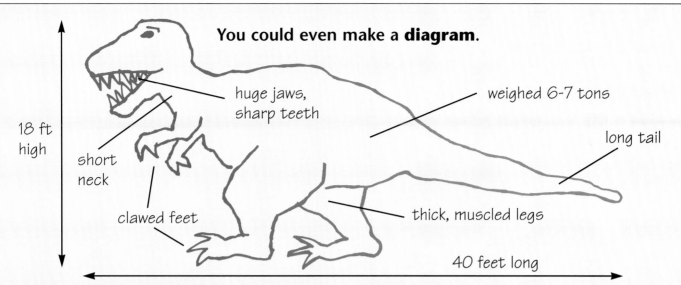

You could even make a **diagram**.

18 ft high

huge jaws, sharp teeth

weighed 6-7 tons

long tail

short neck

clawed feet

thick, muscled legs

40 feet long

A **flow chart** can be useful for showing information in a sequence.

Triassic Period
(230 to 195 million years ago)

Plateosaurus and Melanosaurus lived during the earliest times of the dinosaurs.

↓

Jurassic Period
(195 to 141 million years ago)

Apatosaurus, Stegosaurus, and Brachiosaurus are some of the best-known dinosaurs from this era.

↓

Cretaceous Period
(141 to 65 million years ago)

Tyrannosaurus rex developed during the last of the three periods when dinosaurs lived.

To compare *Tyrannosaurus rex* with other dinosaurs, use a **feature chart** like this:

Dinosaur	Slow Speed	Fast Speed	Short Neck	Eats Meat	Eats Plants	Huge Size
Tyrannosaurus rex	✔		✔	✔		✔
Compsognathus		✔		✔		
Diplodocus	✔				✔	✔
Triceratops	✔		✔		✔	✔

What's the Story?

UNDERSTANDING PLOT

The **plot** is the important events that happen in a story. A story has a **beginning**, a **middle**, and an **end**.

Beginning

You find out what problem the characters have.

Middle

You find out what the characters do to solve their problem.

End

You find out how the characters solve their problem, their solution.

Here's a **story map** about *Henry and Mudge and the Wild Wind.*

Story Map

Characters

Henry
Mudge, his dog
Henry's mother
Henry's father

Setting

Henry's house on a summer's day

Beginning
Problem

Thunderstorms make Henry jumpy and his dog Mudge even jumpier.

Middle
What They Do

During today's thunderstorm, Henry whistles to calm himself. Mudge whines, goes round and round the kitchen table, sits in the bathroom, and hides his head in the couch, but he is still *jumpy.*

End
Solution

Henry tries to calm Mudge by playing a Crawling-Through-Enemy-Lines game with him. Mudge forgets about the storm for a while, but ends up back in the bathroom again. When the sun comes out, Mudge is calm, and the two buddies go out to play under a rainbow sky.

To understand the story plot, ask yourself these questions:

- What problems do the characters have?
- What things do they do to try to solve their problem?
- What is the solution to their problem?

Figure It Out

MAKE INFERENCES AND DRAW CONCLUSIONS

When you make an inference or draw a conclusion, you try to figure out something by using story clues and what you know.

If You Read

Jane was smiling. ⟶ Jane was happy.

The baby wants a bottle. ⟶ The baby is hungry.

Mother took an umbrella. ⟶ Mother expected rain.

You Figure Out

In this story, the author does not tell how Amanda feels about Tweedle-Dee, but you have clues to help you.

TWEEDLE-DEE

"This is my bird, Tweedle-Dee," said Carrie. "I'll let him out so you can meet him."

Amanda didn't want Carrie to open the cage. She said, "Don't bother. I can see him just fine."

"But you have to get to know him," said Carrie. "He's such a sweet bird."

Carrie opened the cage door, and Tweedle-Dee flew out. He circled the room and circled the room again. Then Tweedle-Dee landed right on Amanda's hand.

Amanda didn't move.

"He likes you!" cried Carrie.

"Oh, great," muttered Amanda.

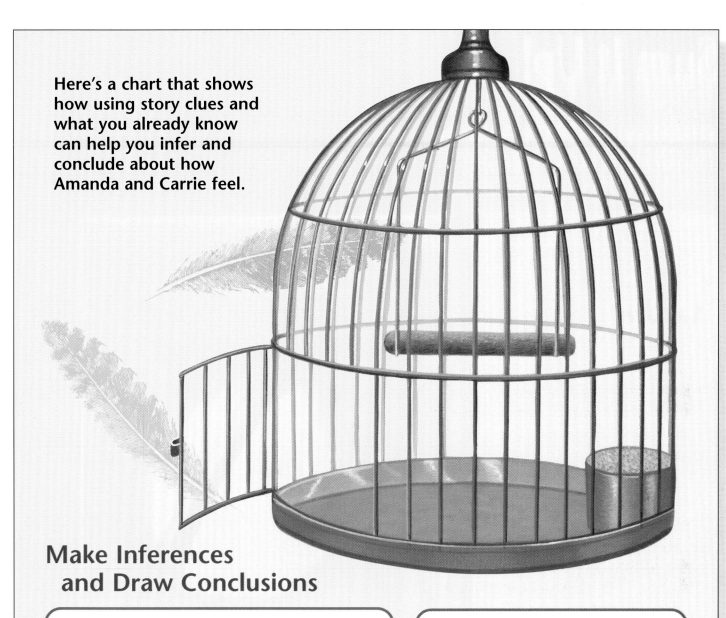

Here's a chart that shows how using story clues and what you already know can help you infer and conclude about how Amanda and Carrie feel.

Make Inferences and Draw Conclusions

Story Clues

Carrie wanted Amanda to meet her pet bird.
Amanda didn't want Carrie to open the cage.
Amanda didn't move when the bird landed on her.
Amanda muttered "Oh, great," when Carrie said the bird likes her.

What You Know

Some people really don't like birds.
Some people are afraid of birds.
Some people are embarrassed to say they don't like someone's pet.

You Infer and Conclude

Amanda is afraid of birds and didn't want Tweedle-Dee near her.
Carrie had no idea how Amanda felt.

Sum It Up!

SUMMARIZE INFORMATION

A **summary** is a short statement that tells about what you read. A summary can tell about all or part of a book.

Here are paragraphs from *A Book About Planets and Stars* by Betty Polisar Reigot.

Saturn

Beautiful Saturn, with its bright rings, is the second largest planet in our solar system. Saturn is almost 10 times bigger than Earth.

Saturn is much, much farther from the sun than Earth. It is very cold out there. And it takes almost 30 of our years for Saturn to go once around the sun.

Like the other very big planets, Saturn is mostly hydrogen and helium.

From far away, Saturn looks yellowish. But close-up photographs taken from the two *Voyager* space probes show it has bands of different colors — pale yellow, golden brown, and reddish brown.

Here is a summary of the paragraphs about Saturn. It includes important information from each of the paragraphs.

Saturn is the second largest planet, and it is farther from the sun than Earth. It is made up of mostly hydrogen and helium and has bands of different colors.

Information from the table of contents is helpful when summarizing a whole book.

NOTE

A **summary** can be about fiction as well. A summary is often included when writing a book report. (*See pp. 62–63.*)

CONTENTS

Here is a summary of *A Book About Planets and Stars* that uses the table of contents.

<u>A Book About Planets and Stars</u> is filled with information and pictures of our solar system. It tells about the inner planets (Earth, Mercury, Venus, Mars) and the outer planets (Jupiter, Saturn, Uranus, Neptune, Pluto). It also includes information about the stars.

What's the BIG Idea?

IDENTIFY MAIN IDEA AND DETAILS

The **main idea** is the most important idea of a paragraph. **Details** are sentences that tell about the main idea.

Sometimes the main idea is **stated** in a sentence at the beginning or the end of a paragraph.

DOLPHIN SOUNDS

Dolphins use sounds to talk with one another. They make whistles, squeaks, and clicks. Scientists study dolphin noises by listening to the patterns of their sounds. They have discovered that each dolphin has a sound of its own that other dolphins use to call it.

The main idea is stated in the first sentence.

Here's a **web** that shows the main idea and details.

Detail
Dolphins make whistles, clicks, and squeaks.

Main Idea
Dolphins use sounds to talk with one another.

Detail
Each dolphin has a sound of its own that other dolphins use to call it.

Detail
Scientists study dolphin noises.

44

Sometimes a paragraph is made up of details about the main idea, but the main idea is **unstated**. The reader needs to look at the detail sentences and figure out the main idea.

Dolphins can tell whether something is near or far away. They talk to other dolphins. They sense when there is danger.

The main idea is not stated.

Detail
They talk to other dolphins.

Main Idea
Dolphins know many things.

Detail
Dolphins can tell whether something is near or far away.

Detail
They sense when there is danger.

EXTRA HELP

When you read, ask yourself these questions:

What are most of the sentences in the paragraph about?

Is there a sentence that tells the main idea?

Which sentences tell about the main idea?

 NOTE

The **topic** of the two paragraphs on these pages is dolphins. Sometimes the topic is called the **subject.**

Why Did the Author Write This?

IDENTIFY AUTHOR'S PURPOSE

Before writing, an author decides on a reason for writing. This reason is called the author's **purpose**.

If you are enjoying what you are reading, one of the author's purposes may be **to entertain**.

If you are learning while you are reading, one of the author's purposes may be **to inform**.

If you are changing the way you think as you read, one of the author's purposes may be **to persuade**.

Entertain

Jack and the Beanstalk
Super Dog to the Rescue
The Giraffe Laughed

Inform

Growing Lima Beans
The Planet Earth
Discover Bees

Persuade

You Can Be a Hero
Plant a Tree
Visit New England

Once upon a time, a boy named Jack planted a bean. A few days later, Jack saw a giant beanstalk that went all the way up to the clouds. He couldn't wait to climb up the beanstalk to find out what was at the top.

This story is fantasy. The author's purpose is to entertain.

Here's how to start a lima bean plant.

First: Put a wet paper towel in a plastic bag.

Next: Put a couple of lima beans on top of the wet paper towel. Close the plastic bag.

Then: Watch the seeds for a few days. Remember to keep the paper towel wet.

Last: See what happens! After the seed sprouts, put your plant in your garden.

This story tells you how to start growing lima bean plants. The author's purpose is to inform.

Try growing your own tree. You'll have fun seeing the small tree grow bigger and taller. Best of all, you will know that you planted something that will be around for a long time and will help the environment, too.

This story tells you to try growing your own tree. The author's purpose is to persuade.

EXTRA HELP

Here are some words to look for when you read. They can help you understand the author's purpose.

NOTE

Often a writer has more than one purpose for writing.

Entertain	Inform	Persuade
Once upon a time. . .	Here are facts about. . .	You must try. . .
Long ago, there lived. . .	Did you know. . .	You would like. . .
The funniest thing was. . .	Here's how to. . .	You should think. . .
In a faraway land. . .	Let's find out about. . .	I think that. . .

Everything Is in Order

IDENTIFY SEQUENCE

Sequence is the order in which events happen in a story. When you identify sequence, you tell the important story events in time order—first, next, and so on.

When you read this story, think about the order in which things happen.

THE FOX AND THE CROW

One day, a hungry fox saw a crow flying overhead. The crow had a big piece of cheese in its beak. The fox wanted that cheese, so it watched the crow.

Soon the crow perched on a tree branch. The fox went over and said to the crow, "I was watching you fly. You certainly are beautiful! A bird as beautiful as you must have a voice that is even more beautiful. I would love to hear you sing."

The crow thought, "That fox is right. I am beautiful, and my voice is beautiful, too."

Then the fox spoke again. "Oh, please sing for me. I want to hear the lovely, clear song that would come from a bird as beautiful as you."

The silly crow began to sing, "Caw! Caw! Caw!" As soon as the crow opened its beak, the cheese fell, right into the mouth of the hungry fox. The fox gobbled up the cheese and ran off, pleased with his slyness. The crow was left without dinner.

A **flow chart** can be used to show the sequence of events in *The Fox and the Crow*.

Flow Chart

First, the fox sees a crow with a big piece of cheese and decides it wants that cheese.

↓

Next, the fox tells the crow how beautiful it is and how much it would like to hear the crow sing.

↓

Then, the crow is flattered into singing. It opens its beak, the cheese falls out, and the fox eats it up.

↓

Finally, the fox goes off, leaving the crow feeling hungry.

EXTRA HELP

When you read, look for these words that signal sequence.

first	next	then
now	last	later
after	before	soon
finally	in the end	
tomorrow		

Why Did That Happen?

UNDERSTAND CAUSE AND EFFECT

The **cause** is the reason something happens.

The **effect** is what happens.

When you read fiction, thinking about **cause and effect** helps you understand why characters do things and why things happen.

Ursula in Yellowstone Park

The car came to a screeching halt. Dad turned and looked at Ursula.

"Why did you scream like that?" he asked.

"Because I thought I saw a bear," said Ursula. "But it was just an old stump."

"Don't do that again," said Dad.

"I won't," said Ursula.

Ursula wanted to see a bear. It was her goal for the week. People didn't see bears in Yellowstone Park very often. But Ursula was sure she would since, after all, her name meant "little bear."

CAUSE ➡ EFFECT

Ursula screams. | Dad stops the car.

CAUSE ➡ EFFECT

Ursula's name means "little bear." | Ursula wants to see a bear.

Knowing Why

It is also important to think about **cause and effect** when you read nonfiction.

Grizzly Bears

Grizzly bears are probably the most dangerous animals in North America. Therefore, people do not like to have them near. Since bears can be harmful to people, bears are chased away from places where people live, or they are moved to wilderness areas. Bears are mostly found in the wild. For this reason, most people have never seen a bear outside a nature park or zoo.

CAUSE	→	EFFECT
Grizzly bears are probably the most dangerous animals in North America.		People do not like having them near.

CAUSE	→	EFFECT
Bears are mostly found in the wild.		Most people have never seen a bear outside a nature park or zoo.

When you read, look for these words that signal cause and effect.

why	because	so
since	therefore	as a result
consequently	due to	for this reason

NOTE

The **effect** is also called the **result**.

What Will Happen Next?

MAKE PREDICTIONS

When you make a prediction, you make a guess about what will happen next, using story clues and what you know.

If you read about a dark sky with flashes of lightning, you might predict that it will rain.

If you read about a hen's egg cracking open by itself, you might predict a baby chick will hatch.

Read about Alex and Beth and think about what will happen next.

Best Friends Forever

It had been three whole days since Alex had waved good-bye to his friend Beth and watched her plane take off. Beth and her family had moved all the way across the United States to California. Alex and Beth had been best friends since kindergarten and he really missed her.

Now Alex sat at the picnic table with a pad of paper and a pen.

What will happen next?

The story clues tell me that Alex missed his friend and had some paper and a pen.

I know that friends often write to friends who live far away.

Prediction: Alex will probably write a letter to Beth.

Alex wrote a long letter to Beth. It was the first letter he had written to her. He wanted to be sure to tell her everything that had happened. He remembered to write about the soccer game their team won, the easy question he got wrong on his history test, and his visit to the dentist—who said Alex would definitely need braces.

Exactly one week later, Alex received a letter back from Beth. He read the letter three times. It ended with "CALL ME!!!" Alex rushed into the kitchen to talk to his mother.

What will happen next?

The story clues tell me that Beth wanted Alex to call her and that Alex went to talk to his mother.

I know that children usually ask permission if they want to call someone who lives far away.

Prediction: Alex will probably ask his mother to help him call Beth.

When you read, stop several times to make predictions. Ask yourself: What will happen next?

On Broadway

STORY SETTING

The **setting** is where and when a story takes place.

The title, the words, and the pictures in a story help you figure out the setting.

Setting
WHERE? New York City
WHEN? Thanksgiving

Thanksgiving Day

It was cold and windy in New York City, but thousands of people came to watch the Thanksgiving Day Parade.

At the Shore

On the morning after Billy's birthday, his mother and father took the whole family to the shore. Billy couldn't wait to get in his new boat.

Setting

WHERE? at the shore
WHEN? on the morning after Billy's birthday

Calm Morning (1904) by Frank Weston Benson

Gift of Charles A. Coolidge Family. Courtesy, Museum of Fine Arts, Boston.

These words tell a story's setting.

Some words tell the place and some words tell the time.

WHERE	WHEN
at the beach	long ago
on the moon	next year
under the bridge	in the year 2000
in back of the house	last night
next to the cave	next winter
at the pond	yesterday
in the desert	at 2 o'clock
near the mountain	once upon a time
at school	January 15th
far away	Wednesday
out in space	on my birthday

NOTE

Sometimes a story has more than one setting. During the story, the time and place may change.

Getting to Know You

STORY CHARACTERS

Characters are the people in a story. Sometimes story characters are animals.

You learn about a character from story clues that tell
- what the character says,
- what the character does,
- what other characters say about the character,
- what the author says about the character.

Story Clues

what the author says

what Hare does

what Hare says

what others say

THE TORTOISE AND THE HARE

One day, a very slow tortoise decided to race a very fast hare.

The race began and Hare smiled and ran off, leaving Tortoise far behind.

"That silly Tortoise can't beat me," said Hare, showing off as usual, and he stopped to sit under a tree.

"Hare is fast, but foolish. Look, Hare has fallen asleep," shouted Skunk as Tortoise crossed the finish line and won the race.

FINISH

Here's a character map that describes what the character is like and how the character feels and acts.

What a Character!

fast runner
One day, a very slow tortoise decided to race a very fast hare.

feels sure of himself
The race began and Hare smiled and ran off, leaving Tortoise far behind.

shows off
"That silly Tortoise can't beat me," said Hare, showing off as usual, and he stopped to sit under a tree.

acts foolishly
"Hare is fast, but foolish. Look, Hare has fallen asleep," shouted Skunk.

HARE

 **EXTRA HELP** Here are some words to use when you describe a character's feelings and actions.

kind	proud	curious	interesting	brave
clever	quiet	powerful	adventurous	happy
stubborn	sad	helpful	silly	shy

Tell It!

RETELL A STORY

When you retell a story, you tell the story in your own words.

Suppose you wanted to retell *Goldilocks and the Three Bears.* You could tell about the characters, use words from the story, and tell what happened in order. You might want to write your ideas on cards to help you cover all the plot details.

Characters

Goldilocks was a very curious little girl.

A Papa, Mama, and Baby Bear lived in a cottage.

Beginning

The Three Bears have porridge that is too hot to eat.

The Three Bears go out.

Goldilocks goes into the house of the Three Bears.

Middle

Goldilocks tries porridge from the three bowls.

She tries out three different chairs.

She tries out three different beds.

Story Words

Papa Bear's _____ was too _____ .

Mama Bear's _____ was too _____ .

Baby Bear's _____ was just right.

End

Goldilocks falls fast asleep.

The Three Bears find Goldilocks fast asleep in Baby Bear's bed.

Goldilocks awakens.

She is frightened and runs home.

58

Story Steps

To help you retell important events from a story, it's good to think of the story as a series of steps. Here is a retelling of *Black Beauty* by Anna Sewell. (Remember to read from the bottom up.)

At the end of the story, Black Beauty is back with Joe Green and dreams about Birtwick.

After that, he had a series of different owners and jobs. The owners he liked best were a family who treated him very kindly.

His next owner caused him to have a serious accident. His legs were never the same and he became a carriage horse.

Black Beauty liked the stable boy, Joe Green, who took care of him. He was sad when his owners moved away and he had to leave Birtwick Park.

His first adventure was on a stormy night when he saved his master's life by not crossing a broken bridge.

When he grew up he was brought to his new home at Birtwick Park, where he met his first friends, Merrylegs and Ginger.

Black Beauty lived with his mother in a grassy meadow.

START HERE

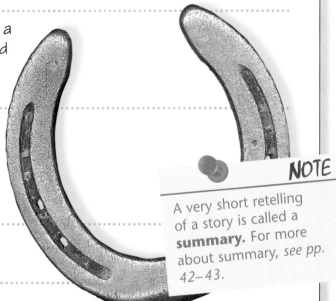

NOTE

A very short retelling of a story is called a **summary**. For more about summary, see pp. 42–43.

What's the Message?

MORAL

The moral is the message the author is trying to give the reader.

Think about how the moral in each of these stories might help someone who hears or reads the story.

In *The Sorcerer's Apprentice*, a young boy who helps a magician does something he has been told not to do. He uses a trick from the magician's secret book to get a broom to carry water. Before he knows it, there are many brooms and he can't stop them. The boy ends up with a flood and more trouble than he can handle. The magician finally rescues him, and the boy learns a lesson.

Moral: When you do what you have been told *not* to do, you may end up in trouble.

In the fable *The Lion and the Mouse*, a little mouse promises that someday she will help a huge lion if he promises not to eat her. The lion lets the mouse go and some days later, when the lion is stuck in a net, the little mouse saves him by eating away at the net.

Moral: Big or small, animals and people can help one another.

In *The Three Little Pigs*, the Third Little Pig, who worked very hard building a house of bricks, was the only pig who was safe from the Big Bad Wolf.

Moral: It is better to work hard and be safe than to play and be sorry.

In *This House is Too Small*, a farmer complains that his house is too small. He is told to bring in animals, a different one each day. The house gets more and more crowded, and so he complains again. Then he is told to take all the animals out. When he does, the house seems quite roomy and the farmer is happy once again.

Moral: Be happy with what you have because things could be worse.

When you read, think about the story's moral.

Ask yourself: What does the author want me to know and think about after I read the story?

Tell All About It!

BOOK REPORTS

You write a **book report** to give information about a book you have read. Sometimes it is helpful to use a form like this. You can add pictures, too.

TELL ABOUT THE BOOK, AND TELL WHY YOU LIKED IT.

My name: Gina B.

Title: Amelia Bedelia and the Baby

Author: Peggy Parish

Illustrator: Lynn Sweat

    This book is about when Amelia Bedelia goes to baby-sit Missy. Amelia Bedelia doesn't know much about babies. She makes a lot of mistakes when she tries to follow Mr. and Mrs. Lane's directions. She makes the wrong kind of food and gives the baby too many baths. Mr. and Mrs. Lane get angry at Amelia Bedelia. But then they see that Missy is fine and that she really likes Amelia Bedelia. Mr. and Mrs. Lane like Amelia Bedelia too and ask her to baby-sit again soon.

    I liked this book because it was fun to read about how Amelia Bedelia gets words mixed up and does silly things.

Or, you might use a form like this:

Putting It Another Way

Title	**Author**	**Illustrator**
Amelia Bedelia and the Baby	Peggy Parish	Lynn Sweat

Setting (where and when)
Mr. and Mrs. Lane's House
afternoon

Characters (who)
Amelia Bedelia   Missy
Mr. Lane   Mrs. Lane

What Happened (Summarize)
In this book Amelia Bedelia goes to baby-sit Missy. Amelia doesn't know anything about babies. As usual, she mixes everything up. She makes supper for the baby, but it is the wrong food. Mr. and Mrs. Lane are mad. Then they see that Missy is all right and she really likes Amelia Bedelia. Mr. and Mrs. Lane like her, too, so they ask Amelia Bedelia to baby-sit again soon.

What You Liked
I like the part about giving the baby two baths.

What You Didn't Like
I didn't think Amelia Bedelia should have given the baby grown-up food.

Why You Would Tell a Friend to Read the Book
If you like Amelia Bedelia, you will love this book. It's so much fun to read about all of her messy mistakes.

Index